KETO PESCATARIAN

COOKBOOK

Over 40 delicious, Quick, and Healthy Recipes For Keto Pescatarian Meals to Burn Layers of Fat and Stay Healthy. Get Low Carbs Meal Plans in Keto Pescatarian Cookbook you can Easily Follow.

Table of Contents

INTRODUCTION

A Keto Pesctarian diet is one that puts an accentuation on plant-based food varieties, fish, and fish may give medical advantages. Fish, similar to meat, is a decent wellspring of protein. However, in contrast to red meat, it's low in immersed fat and regularly wealthy in sound omega-3 unsaturated fats. Fiber is available in plants and is essential to remember for a Keto diet since fiber secures gut microbes, improves stomach related capacity, and forestalls stoppage. In the Keto diet, most of every day calories come from fats, while lesser sums come from proteins. Meat, fish, eggs, and dairy are highlighted vigorously in the Keto diet. Studies show that eating less red meat, or none by any stretch of the imagination, brings down your odds of getting coronary illness and hypertension. Simultaneously, two servings of fish seven days may help your heart.

The omega-3 acids in greasy fish like salmon and mackerel help reduce plaque that develops in courses and lower your chances of getting an unpredictable heartbeat (arrhythmia). Omega-3s additionally lower fatty substance levels in your blood, another reward for heart wellbeing. The solid fats may even positively affect circulatory strain.

Restricting red meat or removing it of our diet totally may likewise bring down your odds of getting malignant growth. One examination shows that pescatarians live more than individuals who follow a diet that incorporates red meat and poultry.

Keto Pescatarian meals

40+ recipes

1. Salmon with Green Beans

Total Time: 35 min| Prep: 20 min. | Bake: 15 min. | Makes: 4 servings

Ingredients

- 4 salmon fillets (6 ounces each)
- 1 tablespoon butter
- 2 tablespoons brown sugar
- 2 tablespoons reduced-sodium soy sauce
- 2 tablespoons Dijon mustard
- 1 tablespoon olive oil
- 1/2 teaspoon pepper

- 1/8 teaspoon salt
- 1 pound fresh green beans, trimmed

Directions

1. Firstly preheat oven to 425°. Place fillets in a 15x10x1-in. baking pan coated with cooking spray. In a small skillet, melt butter; stir in brown sugar, soy sauce, mustard, oil, pepper and salt. Brush half of the paste over salmon.

2. Then place green beans in a large bowl; drizzle with remaining brown sugar mixture and toss to coat. Arrange green beans around fillets. Roast it until fish just begins to flake easily with a fork and green beans are crisp-tender, 14-16 minutes.

2. Keto Naked Fish Tacos

Prep/Total Time: 25 min. | makes: 2 servings

Ingredients

- 1 cup coleslaw blend
- 1/4 cup chopped new cilantro
- 1 green onion, cut
- 1 teaspoon chopped cultivated jalapeno pepper
- 4 teaspoons canola oil, separated
- 2 teaspoons lime juice
- 1/2 teaspoon ground cumin
- 1/2 teaspoon salt, separated
- 1/4 teaspoon pepper, separated
- 2 tilapia filets (6 ounces each)
- 1/2 medium ready avocado, stripped and cut

Directions

1. Spot the initial 4 ingredients in a bowl; throw with 2 teaspoons oil, lime juice, cumin, 1/4 teaspoon salt and 1/8 teaspoon pepper. Refrigerate until serving.

2. Wipe filets off with paper towels; sprinkle with the leftover salt and pepper. In a large nonstick skillet, heat remaining oil over medium-high heat; cook tilapia until fish simply starts to chip effectively with a fork, 3-4 minutes for every side. Top with slaw and avocado.

3.   Sage-Rubbed Salmon

Prep/Total Time: 20 min. | makes: 6 servings

Ingredients

- 2 tablespoons minced new savvy
- 1 teaspoon garlic powder
- 1 teaspoon fit salt
- 1 teaspoon newly ground pepper
- 1 skin-on salmon filet (1-1/2 pounds)
- 2 tablespoons olive oil

Directions

1. Preheat oven to 375°. Blend initial 4 ingredients; rub onto substance side of salmon. Cut into 6 segments.
2. In a large cast-iron skillet, heat oil over medium heat. Add salmon, skin side down; cook 5 minutes. Move skillet to oven; heat just until fish drops effectively with a fork, around 10 minutes.

4. Ginger Scallion Chinese Steamed Whole Fish

Prep Time: 15 minutes | Cooking Time: 12 minutes | Yield: 2 servings

INGREDIENTS:

- 1 whole fish, cleaned
- 1 teaspoon of salt
- 1/2 cup spring onions, chopped into thin strips (divide into 2 parts)
- 2 tablespoons ginger, chopped into thin strips (divide into 2 parts)
- 1/2 cup tamari soy sauce (or use coconut aminos for AIP) (divide into 2 parts)
- 1 tablespoon of avocado oil
- 2 red chilies, sliced (optional - omit for AIP)

- 20 Szechuan peppercorns (optional - omit for AIP)
- 1 tablespoon of sesame oil

DIRECTIONS:

1. Clean the fish (remove scales and remove the insides) (or ask your fishmonger to clean it for you). If desired, you can chop the head off and make it into a fish soup. Cut slits on both sides of the fish and rub in the salt.

2. Transfer the fish to a plate and pour 1/4 cup of the tamari soy sauce (or coconut aminos) on the fish, along with half of the spring onions and ginger. Pour water into your steamer - place the plate in the steamer when the water starts to boil.

3. Steam for 12 minutes.

4. Pour the avocado oil into a skillet over high heat. Add the Szechuan peppercorns, chilies and the rest of the ginger and spring onions.

5. Make the new sauce with the rest of the tamari soy sauce (1/4 cup) and the sesame oil.

6. Remove the steamed fish (discard the sauce the fish was steamed in). Pour the new sauce over the fish, cover with the fried chili, ginger and spring onions and serve.

5. Keto Sardines Salad Recipe

Prep Time: 5 minutes | Cooking Time: 0 minutes | Yield: 1 serving

INGREDIENTS:

- 1 can (120 g) sardines in olive oil or brine, drained
- 1/4 lb. (about 100 g) salad greens
- 1/10 lb. (about 50 g) of deli meat or bacon or leftover meat, chopped fine
- 1 tablespoon (15 ml) of olive oil
- 1 tablespoon (15 ml) lemon juice
- Salt to taste

DIRECTIONS:

1. Prepare the salad greens by tossing them through the olive oil and lemon juice.
2. Add the deli meat and mix.
3. Top with the drained sardines.
4. Sprinkle with salt to taste.

6. Keto Sardines and Onions Recipe

Prep Time: 5 minutes | Cooking Time: 0 minutes | Yield: 1 serving

INGREDIENTS:

- 1 can (100 g) sardines in olive oil
- 1/4 red onion, thinly sliced
- 1 teaspoon (5 ml) apple cider vinegar
- 1 tablespoon (15 ml) of olive oil
- Salt , to taste

DIRECTIONS:

1. Place the sliced onions in the bottom of a bowl. Drizzle with vinegar and olive oil.

2. Top with sardines.

3. Sprinkle with salt to taste.

7. Keto Fried Sardines Recipe with Olives

Prep Time: 0 minutes | Cooking Time: 5 minutes | Yield: 1 serving

INGREDIENTS:

- 1 can (3.5 oz. or 100 g each) sardines in olive oil
- 5 black olives, sliced
- 1 tablespoon (6 g) of garlic flakes
- 1 teaspoon (1 g) parsley flakes
- 1 tablespoon (15 ml) of olive oil , for cooking

DIRECTIONS:

1. Add the tablespoon of olive oil to the skillet and fry everything together for 5 minutes.

8. Lemon Black Pepper Tuna Salad Recipe

Prep Time: 10 minutes | Cooking Time: 0 minutes | Yield: 1 serving

INGREDIENTS:

- 1/3 cucumber, cut into small cubes
- 1/2 small avocado, cut into small cubes
- 1 teaspoon of lemon juice
- 1 can (100-150 g) of tuna
- 1 tablespoon Paleo mayo (use olive oil for AIP)
- 1 tablespoon mustard (omit for AIP)
- Salt to taste
- Salad greens (optional)
- Black pepper to taste (omit AIP)

DIRECTIONS:

1. Mix the diced cucumber and avocado with the lemon juice.

2. Peel the tuna and mix well with the mayo and mustard.

3. Add the tuna to the avocado and cucumber. Add salt to taste.

4. Prepare the green salads (optional: add olive oil and lemon juice to taste).

5. Place the tuna salad on top of the green lettuce.

6. Sprinkle with black pepper.

9. Keto poached egg recipe on smoked haddock and a bed of spinach

Prep time: 10 minutes |Cooking time: 20 minutes | Yield: 2 servings

INGREDIENTS:

- 2 tablespoons (30 ml) of olive oil for cooking
- 1 shallot, peeled and sliced
- 4 oz. (115 g) baby spinach, stalks
- Salt and pepper , to taste
- 2 fillets of smoked haddock (4 oz. / 115 g each), diced (or use smoked salmon)
- 2 large eggs
- Chives cut to garnish

- 1/3 cup (78 ml) Keto Hollandaise sauce (half the recipe there)

DIRECTIONS:

1. Heat the olive oil in a large saucepan over medium heat and add the shallots. After 30 seconds, add the spinach and stir continuously with a wooden spoon. Cook until the spinach has completely shrunk. Season with salt and pepper and set aside to keep warm.

2. At the same time, bring a pan of water to a boil and add the diced haddock, poaching lightly for 8-10 minutes. Drain and set aside to keep warm.

3. To poach the eggs, bring a pot of water to a boil and then simmer. Crack the eggs one at a time in the water and poach them for 4 minutes, then remove with a slotted spoon and set aside on a paper-lined dish. (Simmer the pan with water as you will need it to make the Hollandaise.)

4. For the Hollandaise sauce, beat the 3 egg yolks with the lemon juice in a bowl that you can easily hold over the pan of boiling water. Continue to beat the mixture while holding the bowl over the heat of the boiling water, keeping a close eye on the heat to prevent the eggs from scrambling. Once light and fluffy, add the melted ghee to the eggs 1 tablespoon at a time, whisking continuously until the ghee is completely absorbed and the Hollandaise has thickened.

5. Before serving, divide the warm spinach between two plates and add the diced haddock. Cover with the poached egg and serve with the hollandaise sauce scooped over.

10. Pink Peppercorn Smoked Salmon Salad Recipe

Prep Time: 5 minutes |Cooking Time: 0 minutes | Yield: 1 serving

INGREDIENTS:

- 1 handful of arugula salad leaves
- 1   teaspoons of pink   peppercorns ,   lightly crushed
- 4 olives
- 50 grams of smoked salmon
- 1 slice of lemon

DIRECTIONS:

1. Place the arugula salad leaves and olives in a shallow bowl or plate.

2. Place the smoked salmon on the salad.

3. Sprinkle the lightly crushed pink peppercorns over the smoked salmon.

4. Garnish with a slice of lemon and serve immediately.

11. Paleo Baked Rosemary Salmon Recipe

Prep time: 5 minutes | Cooking time: 30 minutes | Yield: 2 servings

INGREDIENTS:

- 2 salmon fillets (fresh or thawed)
- 1 tablespoon of fresh rosemary leaves
- 1/4 cup (4 tablespoons) of olive oil
- 1 tsp. salt (optional or to taste)

DIRECTIONS:

1. Preheat the oven to 350F (175C).
2. Mix the olive oil , rosemary and salt together in a bowl.
3. Rub the mixture over the salmon fillets.
4. Wrap each fillet in a piece of aluminum foil with some of the remaining mixture.
5. Bake for 25-30 minutes.

12. Creamy Keto Salmon "Pasta" Recipe

Prep Time: 5 minutes | Cooking Time: 5 minutes | Yield: 2 servings

INGREDIENTS:

- 2 tablespoons of coconut oil (30 ml), to boil
- 8 oz. smoked salmon (224 g), diced
- 2 zucchinis (240 g), spiral or use a vegetable peeler to make long noodle-like strands
- 1/4 cup of mayonnaise (60 ml)

DIRECTIONS:

1. Melt the coconut oil in a frying pan over medium heat. Add the smoked salmon and cook until lightly browned, about 2 to 3 minutes.

2. Add the zucchini "noodles" to the pan and cook until soft, about 1 to 2 minutes.

3. Add the mayo to the pan and stir well to combine.

4. Divide the "pasta" between 2 plates and serve.

13. Keto Bacon-Packed Salmon Recipe

Prep time: 10 minutes | Cooking time: 20

minutes | Yield: 2 servings

INGREDIENTS:

- 2 salmon fillets, fresh or frozen (340 g)
- 4 slices of bacon (112 g)
- 1 tablespoon of olive oil (15 ml)
- 2 tablespoons of basil pesto
- 2 tablespoons of paleo Mayo (30 ml)
- Salt and freshly ground black pepper

DIRECTIONS:

1. Preheat the oven to 350 ° F (180 ° C).

2. Pat the salmon dry and wrap in the bacon. Place them on an ovenproof dish and drizzle with the olive oil. Bake for 15-20 minutes.

3. Meanwhile, mix the pesto and mayonnaise together in a small bowl. Season with salt and freshly ground black pepper.

4. When you're ready to serve, top each salmon wrapped in bacon with a dollop of pesto and mayonnaise.

14. Miso Soup Recipes

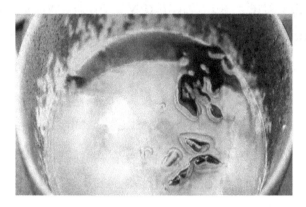

Prep Time: 5 Min| Cook Time: 15 Min | Total Time: 20 Min

INGREDIENTS

- 4 cups water
- 1 piece kombu 4"x6" piece kelp
- 1 ounce katsuobushi bonito pieces
- 3 tablespoon miso paste
- 4 ounces tofu
- 1 tablespoon dried wakame kelp

Directions

1. Wipe the kombu clean with a paper towel. Add the kombu and water to a sauce skillet. Heat to the point of boiling over medium-low heat. At the point when water simply starts to bubble, eliminate the kombu.

2. Bring the kombu water to full bubble. Add the katsuobushi at the same time. Bubble for 60 seconds. Turn heat off and let sit, undisturbed for 10 minutes.

3. meanwhile, dice the tofu. Douse dried wakame in water until extended. channel and dispose of water.

4. In the wake of soaking katsuobushi, the drops will sink to lower part of pot. Strain the katsuobushi through cheesecloth.

5. Return dashi to a stew and promptly turn off heat. Rush in miso paste. At the point when miso has completely broken up, add tofu and wakame

15. Keto Shrimp soup

Preparation: 10 min | Cooking: 10 min | 260 calories |2 servings

Ingredients

- 3 cups   chicken stock
- 80 g rice sticks (noodles)
- carrots, ground
- button (white) mushrooms, daintily cut
- 9 tbsp.   green cabbage, or Savoy, daintily cut
- green onions/scallions, daintily cut
- 14   shrimp, medium-huge
- 1/4 tsp.   gingerroot, ground

- 1 clove   garlic, minced
- 1/2 dried stew peppers, minced
- 2 tbsp.   lime juice, newly crushed
- 2 tsp. fresh cilantro [optional]
- 1 pinch   salt [optional]
- Before you start
- Singular 500 ml (2 cups) serving bowls are required.

Instructions:

1. Cook the rice sticks at that point put in a safe spot.
2. In a pot of salted bubbling water, heat up the shrimp around 3 min, until they become pink. Channel and put in a safe spot.
3. Set up the vegetables. Mesh the carrots, cut the green onions, cabbage, and mushrooms. Part out the vegetables into the individual serving bowls. Add the cooked rice sticks.
4. Heat the stock in a pot. Add the ground ginger, minced garlic and stew pepper. Cook 2 min. Add the cooked shrimp and cook an extra 3-4 min. Change the flavoring.

5. Empty the hot stock into the serving bowls. Add the lime juice, decorate with entire cilantro leaves, and serve.

16. Keto Salmon Fish Cakes Recipe with Creamy Dill Sauce

Prep time: 15 minutes | Cooking time: 20

minutes | Yield: 4 servings

INGREDIENTS:

- **For salmon fish cakes -**
- 3 tins of salmon (approx. 450 g), drained and flaked (or use salmon fillet and cook them first)
- 2 tablespoons of fresh dill (6 g), finely chopped
- 3 medium eggs, beaten
- 1/4 cup of coconut flour (28 g)
- 1/4 cup of grated coconut (20 g)
- 1/4 cup of coconut oil (60 ml)
- Salt and pepper , to taste

For preparing fish cakes -

- 2 tablespoons of coconut oil (30 ml)
- For creamy dill sauce -
- 1/4 cup of mayonnaise (60 ml)
- 1/4 cup of coconut milk (60 ml) (can at room temperature)
- 2 cloves of garlic (6 g), finely chopped or diced
- 2 teaspoons of fresh dill (2 g), chopped
- Salt and pepper , to taste

DIRECTIONS:

1. Beat in a small bowl to combine the dill sauce
2. In a large bowl, mix the fishcake thoroughly. Shape the mixture into 8 patties.
3. In a large skillet, melt 2 tablespoons (30 ml) of coconut oil. Carefully place the patties in the oil in batches. Cook until golden brown on one side then flips and cook until golden brown, about 3 to 4 minutes per side.
4. Serve the salmon patties with the creamy dill sauce.

17. Lemon Garlic Ghee Keto Salmon Recipe with Leeks Asparagus Ginger Bake

Prep time: 10 minutes | Cooking time: 20 minutes | Yield: 2 servings

INGREDIENTS:

- **For the ghee salmon with lemon garlic:**
- 2 salmon fillets (skin on), fresh or frozen (340 g), thaw if frozen
- 1 tablespoon (15 ml) ghee (use avocado oil for AIP)
- 4 cloves of garlic (12 g), chopped
- 2 teaspoons (10 ml) lemon juice
- Salt to taste
- Lemon slices to serve

For the leek, asparagus and ginger roast:

- 10 asparagus (160 g), chopped into small pieces
- 1 leek (90 g), chopped into small pieces
- 2 teaspoons (4 g) ginger powder (or use finely chopped fresh ginger if you have it available)
- Avocado oil or olive oil to fry with
- 1 tablespoon of lemon juice
- Salt to taste

DIRECTIONS:

1. Preheat the oven to 400 F (200 C).
2. Place each salmon fillet on a piece of aluminum foil or baking paper.
3. Divide the ghee, lemon juice and chopped garlic over the two fillets - place on top of the salmon. Sprinkle with some salt. Then wrap the salmon in the foil and place it in the oven.
4. After 10 minutes in the oven, open the foil and bake for another 10 minutes.
5. While the salmon is cooking, put 1-2 tablespoons of avocado oil or olive oil in a skillet and fry the chopped asparagus and leeks over high heat. Bake for 10 minutes and then add the ginger powder, lemon juice and salt to taste. Bake for 1 minute more.

6. Serve by dividing the sauté over 2 plates and placing a salmon fillet on each plate.

18. Garlic Shrimp Caesar Salad Recipe

Prep Time: 15 minutes | Cooking Time: 10 minutes | Yield: 4 servings

INGREDIENTS:

For the shrimp:

- 1 pound shrimp (shell removed)
- 2 tablespoons of olive oil
- 1 tablespoon of lemon juice
- 3 tablespoons of garlic powder
- 1 tablespoon of onion powder
- Salt and pepper

For the salad:

- 1 head of romaine lettuce, chopped
- 1 cucumber, cut into cubes
- For the dressing:

- 1 teaspoon of Dijon mustard
- 1/4 cup Paleo-mayonnaise (you can buy them or make them yourself)
- 1 tablespoon of fresh lemon juice
- 2 teaspoons of garlic powder
- Salt and pepper

For garnish:

- 1 tablespoon of parsley, chopped - for garnish
- 1 tablespoon sliced almonds - for garnish

DIRECTIONS:

1. Preheat the oven to 400F.
2. Mix the shrimps, olive oil, lemon juice, garlic, and onion powder, salt and pepper together. Place the shrimp on the baking tray and roast for 10 minutes.
3. To make the salad dressing, mix together the mayo, mustard, lemon juice, garlic powder, salt and pepper.
4. Toss the dressing with the chopped lettuce, chopped cucumber, and roasted shrimp. Garnish with the chopped parsley and sliced almonds.

19. Keto Salmon Curry Recipe [Paleo, Low Carb]

Prep Time: 10 minutes | Cooking Time: 15 minutes | Yield: 2 servings

DIRECTIONS:

- 1/2 medium onion, diced or finely chopped
- 2 cups (7 oz. or 200 g) green beans, diced
- 1.5 tablespoons (10 g) of curry powder
- 1 teaspoon (3 g) of garlic powder
- Cream the top of 1 (14-oz) can of coconut milk
- 2 cups (480 ml) of bone broth
- 1 lb. (450 g) raw salmon, diced (defrost first if frozen)
- 2 tablespoons (30 ml) of coconut oil for cooking
- Salt and pepper , to taste

- 2 tablespoons of basil (4 g), chopped, for garnish

DIRECTIONS:

1. Cook the diced onion in the coconut oil until translucent.
2. Add the green beans and cook for a few more minutes.
3. Add the stock or water and bring to the boil.
4. Add the curry powder, garlic powder and salmon.
5. Add the coconut cream and simmer until the salmon is tender (3-5 minutes).
6. Add salt and pepper to taste and serve with the chopped basil.

20. Keto Tomato Tuna Bruschetta Recipe

Prep time: 10 minutes | Cooking time: 5 minutes | Yield: 4 servings

INGREDIENTS:

- 4 slices of Keto bread
- 4 tablespoons (60 ml) of olive oil
- 1 6oz (170 g) canned tuna , drained and flaked
- 1 tomato, seeded and cut into small cubes
- 1 tablespoon (15 ml) lemon juice
- 1/4 cup parsley, chopped
- Salt and pepper , to taste

DIRECTIONS:

1. Toast 4 slices of Keto bread.

2. Divide the olive oil over the slices of toast.

3. In a small bowl, combine the tuna, tomato, lemon juice, and parsley. Season with salt and pepper.

4. Drizzle with extra olive oil, if desired.

21. Roasted Cauliflower Broccoli Tuna Bowl

Prep time: 5 minutes | Cooking time: 20 minutes | Yield: 4 servings

INGREDIENTS:

- 1 head of cauliflower, broken into small florets
- 1 cup broccoli, broken into small florets
- Olive oil for cooking
- 1 lemon
- Salt to taste
- Four cans of tuna fish of 150 g (packed in brine, or olive oil)
- 1/4 cup fresh parsley, chopped (or use cilantro)
- For the tahini tamari pasta (omit AIP)
- 1/4 cup of tahini

- 3 tablespoons of gluten-free tamari soy sauce
- 1 tablespoon of sesame oil

DIRECTIONS:

1. Preheat the oven to 400 F (205 C).
2. Place the cauliflower and broccoli florets on a baking tray and drizzle with olive oil. Sprinkle salt and squeeze the juice of 1/4 lemon over the vegetables. Rub the mixture into the vegetables with your hands and spread them on the baking tray.
3. Place in the oven and cook for 20 minutes until the florets are tender and brown on the edges.
4. Let the vegetables cool for a few minutes, then put them in a large bowl and mix with the chopped parsley, 1 tablespoon olive oil, 1/4 lemon juice and extra salt to taste.
5. Mix all the of the pasta well to make the tahini tamari paste.
6. To serve, put the roasted vegetables in a small bowl and cover with a can of tuna. Add some tahini tamari sauce and enjoy.
7. This recipe is enough for 4 people or you can keep the leftover pasta and roasted vegetables in the fridge for future meals.

22. Chinese Petrale Sole Recipe with Ginger and Garlic

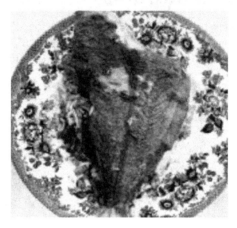

Prep Time: 5 minutes Cooking Time: 15 minutes Yield: 1 serving

INGREDIENTS:

- 1 petrale sole fish
- 2 tablespoons coconut oil (for cooking the fish)
- 3 tablespoons of gluten-free tamari sauce
- 1 teaspoon of white wine vinegar
- 1 tablespoon of spring onions
- 1 teaspoon ginger, grated or chopped
- 3 cloves of garlic, chopped

DIRECTIONS:

1. Place the coconut oil in a skillet over medium to high heat.

2. Place the petrale sole in the skillet and lightly brown each side of the fish for 5 minutes.

3. Add the spring onions, ginger, garlic, tamari sauce and vinegar and cover both sides of the fish with the mixture. Cook for a few more minutes and serve immediately.

23. Mini Fish Cakes Recipe [Paleo, Keto]

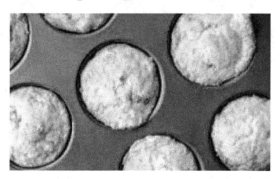

Prep time: 10 minutes | Cooking time: 25 minutes |Yield: 12 mini fish cakes

INGREDIENTS:

- 1-pound white fish, raw and food made into a paste
- 2 cups of almond flour
- 4 eggs, beaten
- Salt and pepper to taste
- 1 teaspoon of white wine vinegar or lemon juice
- 1 teaspoon of baking powder
- 2 tablespoons spring onions or chives, finely chopped
- 1 tablespoon of garlic powder
- 1 tablespoon of ghee or coconut oil (to spread over the cakes before cooking)

DIRECTIONS:

1. Preheat the oven to 375 F (190 C).

2. Mix all *INGREDIENTS:* together in a large mixing bowl.

3. Place muffin liners in a muffin tray and fill each muffin liner with the mixture.

4. Bake for 25 minutes until the mini fish cakes are firm and golden brown on top.

24. Breaded fish recipe (with cod)

Prep time: 10 minutes | Cooking time: 20 minutes | Yield: 4 servings

INGREDIENTS:

- 4 cod fillets (about 0.3 lb. each) (or use other fish)
- 1/2 cup of coconut flour
- 2 tablespoons of coconut flakes
- 3 tablespoons of garlic powder
- 1 tablespoon of onion powder
- Salt to taste
- 2 tablespoons of ghee
- 3 cloves of garlic, chopped
- Coconut oil for greasing baking tray

DIRECTIONS:

1. Preheat the oven to 425F (220C).

2. In a large bowl, combine the breading (coconut flour, coconut flakes, garlic powder, and onion powder). Add salt and taste the mixture to see how much salt you like.

3. Cover a baking tray with aluminum foil and grease with coconut oil .

4. Dip each fish fillet in the breading mixture and cover well. Place the breaded fish on the baking tray.

5. Bake for 15-20 minutes until the fish flakes easily.

6. While the fish is in the oven, prepare the garlic ghee sauce   by melting the ghee a little and adding the chopped garlic.

7. Pour the garlic ghee sauce over the breaded fish and serve.

25. Low Carb Oven Baked Fish

Preparation Time: 25 min |Cooking Time: 20 min |Total Time: 45 min | Servings: 4

INGREDIENTS:

- For breading
- For the eggs
- For the fish
- For the pan

DIRECTIONS:

1. To Prepare: Preheat the oven to 430 ° F. Add a dark colored pan or baking tray to the oven while it heats up - the pan you want to bake the fish in must be hot to melt the butter!

2. Making breadcrumbs: Mix all of them for the breading in a shallow bowl.

3. Preparing eggs: Add the eggs to a SEPARATE shallow dish and beat well.

4. Bread fish: Dip the fish in breadcrumbs to lightly coat it. Then cover the fish with egg. FINALLY, cover the fish with breadcrumbs again, this time you can really grab as much as it sticks! (Just put the breaded pieces of fish on a plate until you've breaded them all.)

5. Melting butter: Take the pan out of the oven VERY CAREFULLY. Add 3 tablespoons of butter to the pan to melt. Divide over the pan and place the pieces of fish on top.

6. Baking: fry the fish for 10 minutes. Flip, add remaining 1 tablespoon butter and cook for 5-10 minutes or until coating are crisp and fish is cooked through.

7. Finish: grill for 2 minutes for a crispy coating. After cooking, let the fish rest on the pan for 2-3 minutes and serve immediately.

26. Keto Creamy Lemon Garlic Salmon

Preparation Time: 5 min |Cooking Time: 20 min |Total Time: 25 min | Servings: 4

INGREDIENTS:

- 4 4 ounces Salmon fillet (skinless or skinless)
- Salt and pepper
- 2 tablespoons avocado oil (click here for my favorite brand on Amazon)
- 1 1/4 cup heavy cream
- 2 tablespoons of lemon juice
- 3 cloves of garlic, chopped
- 2 tablespoons of freshly chopped parsley

DIRECTIONS:

1. Heat the oil in a cast iron skillet over medium heat.

2. Add the salmon fillets skin side up. Cook until the salmon is brown and the fish comes out of the pan easily. Try not to turn early or the salmon will stick.

3. Flip to the other side (the skin side if your salmon has skin) and cook until the salmon skin is crispy and comes out of the pan.

4. Remove the salmon from the pan and set aside.

5. Reduce the heat of the pan to medium heat and whisk together the whipped cream, garlic, parsley, and lemon juice. Simmer for a few minutes to thicken.

6. Season with salt and pepper.

7. Serve the salmon with cream sauce.

27. Easy Keto Baked Tilapia Recipe

Yield: 6 | Preparation Time: 5 mins |Cooking Time: 20 mins |Total Time: 25 mins

INGREDIENTS:

- 1/2 cup of mayo
- 1 teaspoon of garlic, crushed
- 1/4 teaspoon onion powder
- 1/4 teaspoon of salt
- 1/8 teaspoon of pepper
- 1/4 teaspoon of thyme
- 1/4 teaspoon of basil
- 1/2 cup Asiago cheese or Parmesan cheese (grated)
- 6 tilapia fillets or tilapia loin

DIRECTIONS:

1. Preheat the oven to 350 degrees F.

2. Spray a baking sheet or baking dish and put your tilapia fillets in it. Use a paper towel to blot the extra moisture or water off the fillets. This way the mixture will adhere better to the fish.

3. Combine the rest of the in a small bowl and divide between each fillet.

4. Bake for 15-20 minutes or until flaky. If you are using tilapia fillets, it will take closer to 15 minutes and will take longer for the loin. If you want it more brown on top, grill for 2-3 minutes.

28. Coconut Lemongrass Shrimp Soup (Tom Kha Gai)

Prep time: 10 minutes | Cooking time: 30 minutes | Yield: 4 servings

INGREDIENTS:

- 16 Wellness Meats Wild-Caught Raw Brown Shrimp (about 1 pound - these are pretty big shrimp)
- 1 or 2 cups of coconut cream (skim the top of a chilled can of coconut milk - use 1 or 2 cans, depending on how creamy and thick you want the soup)
- 1 liter (32 oz.) of chicken stock
- 3 large mushrooms sliced (traditional recipe uses straw or shiitake)

- 1 lemongrass stalk, split in the center, then chopped into 2-inch pieces
- 1 teaspoon ginger, grated (traditional recipe uses thin slices of galangal)
- 1 small Thai chili (optional)
- 3 tablespoons fish sauce (I use this)
- juice for half a lime
- salt to taste
- 2 tablespoons cilantro, finely chopped (for garnish)

DIRECTIONS:

1. Heat the chicken stock in a medium saucepan and add the lemongrass, ginger, chili, mushrooms, fish sauce, and lime juice.
2. Simmer for 10 minutes.
3. Add the coconut cream and simmer for another 10 minutes until the coconut cream mixes well.
4. Taste the stock and add salt to taste. Add more fish sauce, lime juice or coconut cream, depending on how you like the soup.
5. Add the shrimp and simmer for 8-10 minutes.
6. Serve immediately with the coriander as a garnish.

NUTRITIONAL VALUE:
- Serving Size: 4 bowls

29. Lemon Garlic Fried Shrimp Recipe

Prep Time: 10 minutes | Cooking Time: 10 minutes | Yield: 2 servings

INGREDIENTS:

- 1 lb. (450 g) shrimp, peeled and gutted
- 8 cloves of garlic, chopped
- 1/2 tablespoon of lemon juice
- 2 tablespoons of ghee
- 1/2 teaspoon of salt
- 1/4 teaspoon black pepper
- 2 peppers, chopped
- 4 mushrooms
- 1 zucchini, chopped

DIRECTIONS:

1. Preheat the oven to 400F.
2. Melt the ghee in a bowl and add the chopped garlic, salt and pepper. Divide the mixture in half - keep half of the mixture for serving.
3. Dip each shrimp in half of the mixture and place on skewers.
4. Place the sliced bell pepper, mushrooms and zucchini slices on skewers.
5. Place the skewers on a baking tray and fry the skewers for about 5 minutes on each side.
6. Serve with the preserved garlic ghee mixture.

30. Keto easy seafood soup

Prep/ Total Time: 22 Minutes | 2 Bowls Servings

INGREDIENTS

- 2½ C vegetable stock
- 4 ocean scallops, washed and wiped off
- 2 C gluten free noodles, cooked as coordinated
- carrot, stripped and julienned
- celery ribs, meagerly cut
- red radish, managed and daintily cut
- 1 C spring peas, shelled, pods disposed of
- 2 C shiitake mushroom covers, daintily cut
- 1 scallion, managed and daintily cut
- 2 cloves garlic, shredded
- 1 T new ginger, cleaned and shredded

- 1 T unsalted spread
- 1 T additional virgin olive oil
- 1 tsp. fit salt, more to taste
- run sriracha or other hot sauce
- embellish with sprinkling of miniature greens

DIRECTIONS

1. Wash and afterward strip, trim, cut hack, cut, dice or julienne vegetables as you wish. Wash ocean scallops and afterward wipe off.

2. Empty vegetable stock into a medium-sized pot. Heat to the point of boiling and afterward decrease to stew. Mix in garlic, ginger and salt. Cover.

3. Heat 5 cups of salted water to the point of boiling. Add dried noodles and cook as coordinated. Channel and gap into two soup bowls.

4. Simultaneously, carry a medium measured skillet to medium-high temperature. Add spread and olive oil, permitting them to mix and come to temperature. Add scallops, being mindful so as not to swarm them in the skillet. Burn one side, around 3-4 minutes, turn over

and rehash. When cooked, eliminate from skillet and permit to rest.

5. Return stock to a bubble. Add vegetables and cook for 4 minutes.

6. Using an opened spoon, eliminate the entirety of the vegetables from the stock. Spoon onto cooked noodles, partitioning them uniformly between the two dishes.

7. Move two singed scallops into each bowl. Spoon equivalent measures of bubbling stock into each bowl.

8. Add a scramble of hot sauce to each bowl and trimming both with a sprinkling of micro greens.

31. Popcorn Shrimp Recipe [Dairy Free, Nut Free]

Prep time: 5 minutes | Cooking time: 20 minutes | Yield: 2 servings

INGREDIENTS:

- 1/2-pound small shrimp, peeled
- 2 eggs, beaten
- 6 tablespoons of paleo Cajun seasoning (recipe here)
- 6 tablespoons of coconut flour
- coconut oil for baking

DIRECTIONS:

1. Melt the coconut oil in a saucepan (use enough coconut oil so it's 1/2 inch deep) or deep-fry.

2. Place the beaten eggs in a large bowl and mix the coconut flour and spices and place in another large bowl.

3. Drop a handful of shrimps into the beaten eggs and stir around so that each shrimp is covered.

4. Then remove the shrimps from the beaten eggs and put them in the spice bowl. Brush the shrimps with the coconut flour and spice mixture.

5. Place the coated shrimp in the oil and fry until golden brown. Try not to stir the pan or put too many shrimps in the pan at once (make sure all shrimp touch the oil).

6. Use a slotted spoon to remove the shrimp and place them on a paper towel to absorb the excess oil. Repeat for the rest of the shrimp (change the oil if there are too many solids in it).

7. Let cool for 10 minutes (the outside will be crispy) and enjoy on its own or with some Paleo ketchup.

32. Keto Shrimp Fried Rice Recipe

Prep Time: 10 minutes | Cooking Time: 15 minutes | Yield: 2 servings

INGREDIENTS:

- 1/2-pound shrimp (225 g), peeled and deveined
- 1/2 cauliflower flour (300 g)
- 1 carrot (50 g), cut into cubes
- 4 tablespoons (60 ml) avocado oil for cooking
- 2 tablespoons (30 ml) gluten - free tamari sauce
- 1 teaspoon of sesame oil (5 ml)
- 2 cloves of garlic (6 g), finely chopped
- 2 spring onions (10 g), chopped for garnish
- Salt to taste

DIRECTIONS:

1. Add avocado oil to a frying pan and fry the shrimp until tender. Put them on a plate to set aside.

2. Break the cauliflower into florets, pat dry and process into small rice-like particles. If it is slightly wet, squeeze out the excess water with your hands or a kitchen towel. This prevents the rice from turning into mush.

3. In the same pan, cook the rice and carrots until tender (or to your liking). Then add the shrimp back to the pan.

4. Add the tamari sauce, sesame oil, garlic and cook over high heat for 1-2 minutes. Add salt to taste.

5. Divide between 2 plates, garnish with chopped green onions and serve.

33. Asian Keto Miso Soup Recipe (Topped with Shrimp)

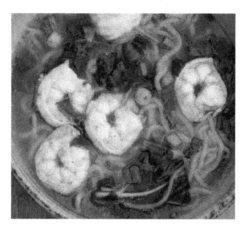

Prep Time: 10 minutes | Cooking Time: 0

minutes | Yield: 2 servings

INGREDIENTS:

- 2 (85 g) cartons of shirataki noodles, drained
- cups of chicken broth (600 ml) and bone broth
- 1 tablespoon of tahini sauce (15 ml)
- 1 tablespoon of gluten - free tamari sauce or coconut aminos (15 ml)
- 1/2-pound shrimp (225 g), peeled
- 1 teaspoon of sesame oil (5 ml)
- 2 tablespoons of lemon juice (30 ml)
- 2 green onions (10 g), sliced diagonally
- 1 cup of spinach (30 g), thinly sliced

- Pinch of hot sauce (optional)

DIRECTIONS:

1. Rinse the shirataki noodles well, following the package *DIRECTIONS:* to remove the odor. It also helps to boil it up a bit and then rinse it off again. Drain and set aside.

2. Heat the stock and add the tahini sauce and tamari sauce. Once steamed, add the shrimp, sesame oil, and lemon juice and keep the heat until you're sure the shrimp are cooked.

3. Add the drained noodles along with the green onions and thinly sliced spinach to the stock and heat through.

4. Divide between 2 bowls and serve immediately with a splash of hot sauce.

34. Keto Shrimp And Grits

Preparation Time: 10 mins |Cooking Time: 15 mins |Yield: 4 Servings

INGREDIENTS:

- 2 tablespoons (30 ml) of olive oil for cooking
- 4 slices of bacon, cut into cubes
- 10 white mushrooms (100 g), quartered
- 1 green onion, finely chopped
- 2 cloves of garlic, peeled and finely chopped
- 1/2 lb. (225 g) shrimp, peeled and cleaned
- 2 tablespoons (30 ml) of lemon juice
- 1 cup (240 ml) coconut cream
- 3/4 cup (60 g) shredded coconut

- 2 tablespoons (2 g) of fresh parsley, finely chopped for garnish
- Salt and pepper , to taste

DIRECTIONS:

1. Add olive oil to a pan and fry the bacon until crispy.
2. Leave the fat in the pan and cook the mushrooms and onions in the pan until caramelized, add the garlic halfway through. Remove from pan and set aside to keep warm.
3. Place the shrimp in the same pan (you may need to add another dash of olive oil) and fry the shrimp until pink and cooked through. Add the lemon juice and season with salt and pepper. Then add the cooked shrimp to the mushroom mixture.
4. In a small pan, heat the coconut cream and then add the grated coconut. Cook to a thick porridge-like consistency.
5. Divide the coconut grits among four small bowls. Spoon over the shrimp mixture, sprinkle with the crispy bacon and garnish with finely chopped parsley.

35. Keto Coconut Shrimp Recipe

Prep time: 10 minutes | Cooking time: 5 minutes | Yield: 2 servings

INGREDIENTS:

- 3 tablespoons of coconut flour (21 g)
- 1 medium egg (44 g), beaten
- 1/2 cup of coconut (32 g)
- 7 oz. raw peeled shrimp (196 g)
- oil, for frying
- salt and freshly ground black pepper
- lime wedges, to serve

DIRECTIONS:

1. Line a tray or plate with paper towels. Put aside.
2. Prepare three bowls. Put the coconut flour in a bowl, the beaten egg in the second and the coconut flakes in the last.
3. Toss all of the shrimp into the coconut flour. Take one shrimp one at a time and dip them in the egg so that the excess water can run off. Then dip the shrimp in the coconut and press the coconut firmly into the shrimp.
4. Heat enough oil to fry the shrimp. Once warm, fry the shrimp for a minute or two, then remove with a slotted spoon and place on your tray or plate.
5. Season with salt, pepper and a good squeeze of lime. Serve warm.

36. Keto Shrimp Cocktail Recipe

Prep Time: 5 minutes | Cooking Time: 5 minutes | Yield: 2 servings

INGREDIENTS:

- 2 tablespoons (30 ml) Keto Tomato Ketchup Recipe
- 2 tablespoons (30 ml) mayonnaise
- Salt and freshly ground black pepper , to taste
- 8 oz. cooked, peeled shrimp (1/2 lb. or 225 g)
- 1 cup iceberg lettuce, shredded
- 1/2 large avocado, diced
- Squeeze Italian herbs to taste
- 2 teaspoons (10 ml) lemon juice
- Lemon wedges, to serve

DIRECTIONS:

1. Combine the tomato ketchup with the mayonnaise. Season with salt and pepper. Coat the shrimps with this sauce.

2. Divide the shredded lettuce and diced avocado among two cocktail glasses or bowls. Finish with the shrimp. Squeeze 1 teaspoon of lemon juice over each glass.

3. Serve with lemon wedges and sprinkle a pinch of Italian herbs over the shrimp.

37. Keto Shrimp and Cucumber Appetizer Recipe

Prep Time: 10 minutes | Cooking Time: 10 minutes | Yield: 6 servings

INGREDIENTS:

- 2 cucumbers, each chopped into 5 sections (1.5 inches wide per section)
- 12 shrimp, boiled
- 1/4 onion, diced
- 1 chili pepper, seeded and diced
- 1 tomato, diced
- Salt and pepper , to taste
- 3 tablespoons (45 ml) of olive oil , for drizzling

DIRECTIONS:

1. Divide the top of each cucumber piece in eight so that you can put the sauce and shrimp on top.

2. Make the sauce by mixing the onion, bell pepper, tomato and salt and pepper in a small bowl.

3. Spoon some of the sauce onto each cucumber portion.

4. Then divide a shrimp over each section and drizzle with olive oil.

38. Low Carb Keto Jambalaya Recipe

Preparation time 10 minutes | Cooking time 20 minutes | Total time 30 minutes | Servings 6 servings

INGREDIENTS:

- 2 tbsp. Olive oil
- 1 pound Andouille sausage (thinly sliced)
- 2 large peppers (diced; I used red and green)
- 1/2 large onion (diced)
- 1/2 cup celery (diced)
- 4 cloves of garlic (finely chopped)
- 1 lb. large shrimp (peeled and thawed, thawed if frozen)
- 2 pounds cauliflower rice (fresh or frozen)
- 1 14.5 oz. tin diced tomatoes (drained)

- 1/4 cup of chicken stock
- 2 tbsp. Cajun (start with 1 tbsp. if you don't want spicy)
- 1 teaspoon sea salt (to taste)
- Green onions (sliced; optional, for garnish)
- Fresh parsley (chopped; optional, for garnish)

DIRECTIONS:

1. Heat the oil in a large frying pan over medium heat. Add the bell pepper, onions and celery. Bake for 5-8 minutes, until the vegetables are soft.

2. Add the sliced sausage. Bake for about 5 minutes, until brown.

3. Make a well in the center and add the chopped garlic. Let it sizzle for about 30 seconds, until fragrant, and then stir in with everything else.

4. Add the cauliflower rice, diced tomatoes, bone stock and Cajun seasoning. Stir well and then add the shrimp. Increase heat to high to bring to a boil, and then continue to simmer uncovered, stirring occasionally, until cauliflower is tender, shrimp is tender and liquid has reduced, about 5-7 minutes. It will release more liquid at first and then decrease in volume again as it simmers more.

5. Then Season with salt to taste and / or more Cajun seasoning if you like. Garnish with green onions and parsley if desired.

39. Napa Cabbage Soup with chicken Meatballs and seafood shrimps

Prep time: 5 min | Cook time: 25 min |

Serving 2-4

Ingredients

Soup base

- 2 large slices ginger
- 3 to 4 green onions , chopped
- (Option 1) Quick pork and chicken broth
- 1/4 cup chopped pancetta (or bacon)
- cup chicken stock (or 2 cups, if you want the soup to be extra rich) (Optional)

(Option 2) Clear seafood broth

- 1/4 cup dried shrimp
- 1/4 cup dried scallops
- (Option 3) Easy broth
- cups chicken stock (or pork stock)

Meatballs

- 1/2 pound (230 grams) ground turkey (or ground pork)
- 1/4 cup finely chopped green onion (green part) (Optional)
- 1 tablespoon Shaoxing wine (or dry sherry or Japanese sake)
- teaspoons or tamari for gluten-free
- 2 teaspoons potato starch
- 1 teaspoon ginger , grated
- 1 large egg
- 1/4 teaspoon salt
- 1 teaspoon sesame oil (or peanut oil, or vegetable oil)

Soup base

- 2 enormous cuts ginger
- to 4 green onions , chopped
- (Alternative 1) Quick pork and chicken stock
- 1/4 cup chopped pancetta (or bacon)

- 1 cup chicken stock (or 2 cups, in the event that you need the soup to be additional rich) (Optional)

(Alternative 2) Clear fish stock
- 1/4 cup dried shrimp
- 1/4 cup dried scallops
- (Alternative 3) Easy stock
- 3 cups chicken stock (or pork stock)

Meatballs
- 1/2 pound (230 grams) ground turkey (or ground pork)
- 1/4 cup finely chopped green onion (green part) (Optional)
- 1 tablespoon Shaoxing wine (or dry sherry or Japanese purpose)
- 2 teaspoons or tamari for sans gluten
- 2 teaspoons potato starch
- 1 teaspoon ginger , ground
- 1 huge egg
- 1/4 teaspoon salt
- 1 teaspoon sesame oil (or nut oil, or vegetable oil)
- Soup

- to 8 huge Napa cabbage leaves , chopped (create 6 to 8 cups)
- 1/2 daikon radish, stripped and chopped (creates 2 cups) (Optional)
- 1 clump enoki mushrooms brilliant needle mushrooms, intense closures eliminated and isolated
- 1/2 (400g/14-ounces) block delicate tofu , chopped
- Ocean salt to taste

Directions

1. Soup base alternative 1 - Quick pork and chicken stock
2. Heat a 3.8-liter (4-quart) pot over medium heat and add the greasy pieces of the pancetta. At the point when it begins to sizzle, go to medium low heat. Blending once in a while, cook until the fat renders and the pancetta becomes brilliant.
3. Add the lean pieces of the pancetta. Keep cooking and blending until brown.
4. Add chicken stock and promptly utilize a spatula to scratch the brown pieces off the

lower part of the pot. Add 2 cups water (add 1 cup water, if using 2 cups chicken stock; or 3 cups water + 1 tablespoon shellfish sauce or hoisin sauce, in the event that you would prefer not to utilize chicken stock), ginger, and green onion. Cook over high heat until bubbling. Go to medium low heat. Cover and bubble for 5 minutes.

5. Soup base choice 2 - Clear fish stock

6. Flush dried scallops. Spot scallops in a little bowl and add water to cover. Rehydrate for 2 to 3 hours. Channel and attack little pieces.

7. Wash dried shrimp, move to a little bowl, and add water to cover. Rehydrate for 30 minutes. Channel and put in a safe spot.

8. Join the rehydrated scallops and shrimp, ginger, green onion, and 3 cups water in a 3.8-liter (4-quart) pot. Heat over high heat until bubbling. Go to medium heat. Cover and let stew for 5 minutes.

9. Soup base alternative 3 - Easy stock

10. Join chicken stock (or pork stock), ginger, and green onion in a 3.8-liter (4-quart) pot. Heat over high heat until bubbling. Go to

medium heat. Cover and bubble for 5 minutes.

Meatballs

11. Consolidate every one of the ingredients for the meatballs in an enormous bowl. Mix until all ingredients are simply joined and structure a somewhat runny blend. Don't over-mix it. Let sit for 5 to 10 minutes.

Soup

12. Wash and cut veggies while letting the stock stew.

13. Add daikon radish into the soup pot. Cover and cook for 5 minutes.

14. Add the thick pieces of the Napa cabbage. Cover and cook for 5 minutes.

15. Add the green pieces of the Napa cabbage and enoki mushroom into the soup. Cook for 2 to 3 minutes.

16. You can change the flavoring now, by adding somewhat salt, if necessary.

17. Add delicate tofu. Push every one of the ingredients aside of the pot, to clear some space for the meatballs. (On the off chance that you need more space in the pot, you can

take out a portion of the Napa cabbage leaves)

18. Utilize a spoon to scoop 1 to 1.5 tablespoons of the meatball blend and cautiously add it into the soup. Rehash this until you've made around 15 meatballs.

19. Cover the pot and stew until the meatballs are simply cooked through, 4 to 5 minutes. Mood killer heat promptly and eliminate the pot from the oven, keeping it covered.

20. Serve hot as a principle or side. To make it a full dinner, you can heat up certain noodles (or mung bean noodles or shirataki noodles) and add them into the soup toward the finish of cooking. For this situation, you should add a smidgen more salt or light soy sauce, to make the stock somewhat saltier. Thusly, it will taste perfectly with the noodles.

40. Shrimp Rangoon Mini Paprika

Preparation Time: 30 min |Cooking Time: 10 min |Total Time: 40 min

INGREDIENTS:

- 15 mini peppers cut in half, seeds and pith removed
- ½ lb. raw shrimp peeled, tail removed, gutted
- 1 teaspoon chili powder
- ¼ teaspoon of garlic powder
- ¼ teaspoon of salt or more to taste
- 1 tablespoon of olive oil
- 120ml room temperature cream cheese (full fat is best, but light cream cheese will work too)
- 2 tablespoons of chopped green onions
- 1 teaspoon of lime juice

- ⅓ cup of finely chopped Gouda or white Cheddar cheese (about 3 ounces)
- olive oil spray or extra olive oil for brushing the baking tray

DIRECTIONS:

1. Preheat the oven to 350F. Spray a large baking sheet with nonstick cooking spray or brush with olive oil.
2. In a medium bowl, combine the shrimp, chili powder, garlic powder, and salt. Mix well. Heat the olive oil in a large frying pan and cook the shrimp over high heat for 2 minutes per side, or until tender. Set aside to cool.
3. Coarsely chop the cooked shrimp into small pieces.
4. In a medium bowl, combine the chopped shrimp, room temperature cream cheese, chopped green onions, and lime juice. Mix well. Taste it and add salt and pepper if necessary.

5. Fill each bell pepper half with about ½ - 1 tablespoon of the cream cheese mixture and press down gently to fill the bell pepper. Place the mini peppers on the baking tray. Sprinkle a pinch of grated cheese on each mini pepper. Bake at 350F for 10 minutes. Remove from heat and let cool 10 minutes before serving.

41. Wonton Soup with shrimps

Prep Time: 1 HOUR| Cook Time: 5 MINUTES |

Total Time: 1 HOUR 5 MINUTES

| Servings: 8 servings

Ingredients

- pack wonton coverings (80 coverings)
- Filling
- 1/2 lbs. (230 g) ground lean pork
- 1/2 lbs. (230 g) stripped shrimp, chopped into little pieces
- 1 tablespoon finely minced ginger
- green onions , finely chopped
- 1 tablespoon light soy sauce (or soy sauce)
- tablespoons Shaoxing wine (or dry sherry)
- 1/2 teaspoon salt

- 2 tablespoons sesame oil
- (Alternative 1) Chicken soup base
- 8 cups chicken stock
- 8 teaspoons light soy sauce (or soy sauce)
- 8 teaspoons minced ginger
- 8 teaspoons sesame oil
- Salt , to taste
- (Choice 2) Chinese road style soup base
- 8 cups hot stock from the wonton bubbling water
- 8 tablespoons papery dried shrimp , or to taste
- 8 major bits of dried ocean growth for soup , arranged by guidance
- teaspoons chicken bouillon
- 8 teaspoons light soy sauce , or to taste
- 8 teaspoons sesame oil
- Garnishes
- green onions , chopped
- 4 stalks infant bok choy , slice to reduced down (or 4 cups infant spinach)
- 1 bunch cilantro, chopped (Optional)
- Hand crafted stew oil , to taste (Optional)

Directions

Make the filling

1. Without a food processor: Combine ground pork, shrimp, ginger, green onion, soy sauce, Shaoxing wine, salt and sesame oil in a major bowl. Blend well in with a fork until everything consolidates well together and the combination feels somewhat tacky.

2. With a food processor or a blender: coarsely cleave the ginger and green onion. Add all the filling ingredients with the exception of the shrimp. Blend until it frames a velvety paste. Add the shrimp and mix once more, until the shrimp are finely chopped however don't turn into a paste.

3. Wrap the wonton

4. To make wontons, place a wonton covering in one hand, scoop a teaspoon of wonton filling and spot it close to the restricted side of the wonton covering (you can add more filling to the wonton on the off chance that you like, as long as you can in any case wrap it). Overlap the restricted side over the filling; at that point roll the filling right through the opposite side of the covering. Tie the two finishes and press

together to bolt the filling inside the covering. Brush a dainty layer of water onto the wonton covering and press the closures together.

5. Make each wonton in turn, and line up every one of the wontons on a major wooden cutting board. In the event that you're not going to heat up the wontons promptly, utilize a moist paper towel (or cheesecloth) to cover the wontons to keep them from drying out.

6. On the off chance that you're not going to heat up the wontons that very day, place them in a water/air proof holder with a few layers of wet paper towels on the base. Thusly, they can be put away in the cooler for as long as 2 days.

(Alternative 1) Make the chicken soup base

7. Consolidate the chicken stock, ginger, and soy sauce in a pot. Heat to the point of boiling. Let bubble for 10 minutes. Go to least heat to keep warm and begin cooking wontons (see beneath).

8. Plan 8 medium-sized dishes. Add the cooked wontons and bok choy. Add 2 tablespoons green onion, 1 tablespoon soy sauce and 1/2 teaspoon sesame oil into each bowl. Pour in 1

and 1/2 cups hot stock. Trimming with cilantro and stew oil, if using.

9. Serve hot.

(Alternative 2) Make the road seller style soup base

10. To get ready 1 serving of wonton soup base, add a major spoon of cilantro, 1 tablespoon papery dried shrimps, a liberal piece of dried kelp, 1/4 teaspoon chicken bouillon, and some child bok choy into a major bowl. Rehash the interaction to set up the remainder of the soup base in the other serving bowls. Cook wontons (see beneath).

11. To make 1 serving of wonton soup, utilize a spoon to move cooked wontons, bok choy, and the hot soup into a serving bowl with every one of the ingredients from the past advance. Sprinkle 1 teaspoon soy sauce and 1 teaspoon sesame oil into the bowl and give it a delicate mix. The soup ought to be golden hued. Add additional soy sauce or salt if the soup isn't sufficiently pungent. Dissipate green onion on

top. Enhancement with cilantro and stew oil, if using.

12. Serve hot.

Heated up the wonton

13. To heat up the wontons, heat a major pot of water until bubbling. Add 10 to 20 wontons all at once and bubble over medium heat until wontons are drifting on the outside of the water.

14. Keep on bubbling until the coverings are swollen, around 1 to 2 minutes for little wontons and 2 to 3 minutes for greater ones. Take a wonton out with an opened spoon and split it with a chopstick or fork. On the off chance that the wonton is cooked through, stop heat quickly and move the wontons to singular serving bowls. If not, keep on bubbling until cooked through.

15. Whenever you've cooked the wontons, add the bok choy. Let cook until delicate. Eliminate from the pot, channel well, and put in a safe spot.

To cook frozen wontons

16. Heat a huge pot of water to the point of boiling over high heat. Add wontons. Mix tenderly to keep from staying. Cook until heating the water to the point of boiling once more. Go to medium-low heat. Cover the pot with a little hole on one side, to forestall spilling. Keep bubbling for 2 minutes (3 minutes for bigger wontons). Remain adjacent to the pot the entire chance to screen the stock. On the off chance that the stock begins to spill, reveal and mix, and supplant the cover. Uncover and keep cooking for one more moment, or until the wontons are cooked through.

17. There are numerous kinds of dried ocean growth. My unique formula utilized a sort of moment ocean growth that will rehydrate quickly once positioned into the hot soup. There are different kinds of fish that require some splashing prior to using. Peruse the rear of your bundle and adhere to the guidelines as needs be.

18. The sustenance realities for this formula are determined dependent on 1 bowl of chicken-stock based soup containing 10 wontons.

42. Low Carb Bacon Pineapple Shrimp Skewers

Start to finish: 35 minutes Servings: 3 (for 6 large skewers)

INGREDIENTS:

- 18 medium or large wild caught shrimp
- 9 slices of uncured meadow bacon, cut in half and precooked (but still pliable)
- 1 1/2 cups organic pineapple chunks (24 pieces)
- 2 tablespoons grass-fed butter or ghee , melted
- 1 teaspoon of dried oregano
- 3/4 teaspoon flaky sea salt
- Optional: fresh parsley for garnish

DIRECTIONS:

1. Preheat the grill over medium heat.
2. Wrap each shrimp with a piece of partially cooked bacon and set aside.
3. Assemble Shrimp Skewers: Alternate pineapple chunks with bacon-wrapped shrimp on each skewer. You should have 6 skewers, each with 3 shrimp and 4 pieces of pineapple. Put aside.
4. In a small bowl, combine melted butter or ghee, dried oregano, and flaky sea salt. Generously brush each shrimp skewer, front and back, with butter mixture.
5. Grill for about 2 minutes on each side or until shrimp are opaque and cooked through. Brush with more butter, garnish with chopped parsley, if desired, and serve.

43. Mussels with Miracle Noodle Angel Hair

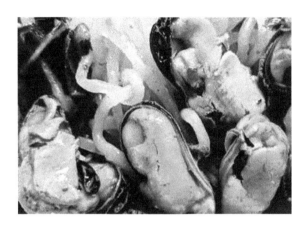

Prep time: 30 min | Servings: 2

INGREDIENTS:

- lb. of fresh mussels, scrubbed and de-bearded, removed from shells and rinsed thoroughly
- 1 cup of Swiss chard (or dark leafy greens of your choice), chopped
- packets of Miracle Noodle Angel Hair Pasta
- tablespoons of Kerry gold butter
- 1/4 cup of dry white wine
- 1 tablespoon of lemon thyme, fresh
- 1 tablespoon flat-leaf Italian parsley, fresh
- 1/2 cup of freshly-grated Parmesan cheese

- Squeeze of lemon, fresh Optional: red pepper flakes

DIRECTIONS:

1. Melt the coconut oil in a saucepan (use enough coconut oil so it's 1/2 inch deep) or deep-fry.

2. Place the beaten eggs in a large bowl and mix the coconut flour and spices and place in another large bowl.

3. Drop a handful of shrimps into the beaten eggs and stir around so that each shrimp is covered.

4. Then remove the shrimps from the beaten eggs and put them in the spice bowl. Brush the shrimps with the coconut flour and spice mixture.

5. Place the coated shrimp in the oil and fry until golden brown. Try not to stir the pan or put too many shrimps in the pan at once (make sure all shrimp touch the oil).

6. Use a slotted spoon to remove the shrimp and place them on a paper towel to absorb the excess oil. Repeat for the rest of the shrimp (change the oil if there are too many solids in it).

7. Let cool for 10 minutes (the outside will be crispy) and enjoy on its own or with some Paleo ketchup.

44. Keto Copycat Zucchini Noodles With Shrimp

INGREDIENTS

- 1/3 cup of lemon juice
- 5-zucchini
- 2-tablespoons of unsalted butter
- 2-tablespoons of chopped fresh parsley
- 2-tablespoons of olive oil
- 2-tablespoons of chopped garlic
- 3-teaspoons lemon zest
- ½ teaspoon of red pepper

DIRECTION

1. Make zucchini zoodles with a spiralizer.
2. Season the shrimp with salt and black pepper.
3. Heat the butter and oil together in a pan over medium heat. Once the butter has melted, upload the garlic and shrimp.
4. Cook the shrimp for two to three minutes, until the red and cooked through. Remove and reserve.
5. Add the vermouth and lemon juice to the butter mixture and simmer for one to two minutes.
6. Add the lemon zest, pink pepper, and chopped fresh parsley. Add the zucchini and cook for another minute until the zoodles are barely soft and protected with the sauce.

Conclusion

I would like to thank you all for choosing this book. Hope you all enjoyed easy Keto pasctarian diet meals recipes. Pasctarian meal eating habits revolve around keeping the diet in balance. Trying these delicious meals full of nutrients at home will be an awesome idea for those people who want to take a considerable amount of nutrients.

I wish you all good luck

CPSIA information can be obtained
at www.ICGtesting.com
Printed in the USA
BVHW051007090821
613981BV00002B/78